Telling the Truth with a Smile

GOLF STORIES from the BUCK CREEK SERIES

I hope you laugh w/ me as much as at me!

10.1.18

JERRY PATTENGALE

dustjacket

Telling the Truth with a Smile: Golf Stories from the Buck Creek Series / Jerry Pattengale

ISBN: 978-0-9969958-6-3

Dust Jacket Press
PO Box 721243
Oklahoma City, OK 73172

www.DustJacket.com
Info@DustJacket.com

Cover and Interior Design by D.E. West / ZAQ Designs
Printed in the United States of America

dustjacket
www.dustjacket.com

DEDICATION

To Jordan Spieth and Austin Conroy—two great golfers. One gets paid by the PGA to golf, the other by Indiana Wesleyan University to coach students on the golf course. Both have become role models on and off the short grass. And both could beat me with a putter and any other club.

And to Chris Faulkner. He plays golf with the same intensity he played professional football—especially in the sand traps.

All proceeds from this book's first printing go to Lightriders Ministries in honor of the late Paul E. Turner

CONTENTS

INTRODUCTION

The golf course: it's that rare place where one minute four guys are concentrating on their target, taking aim, and swinging for glory, but minutes later they're in the fetal position, rolling on the tee station laughing. Grown men become silly. Young men and women witness transformations of fathers into man-boys.

This little book captures a hilarious glimpse into the human condition. Whether we know the golfer who just beaned the clubhouse or the one who put a few balls into the pond before tossing in his wedge, we offer empathetic laughs all the same.

Here I offer some true stories culled from my journey from Buck Creek, Indiana, to the present. The opening chapter won some acclaim for categorizing familiar mis-hits with familiar faces. The last chapter, written a few days after surviving quadruple bypass surgery, reflects my empathy with Jordan Spieth's water balls on hole 12 of the 2016 Masters. Between these bookends, you'll find reflections from my childhood, college-age years, and more recently in my fifties—golf stories that have framed my life.

The last time I kept my PGA handicap it was 10.5. Unfortunately, my best club doesn't factor in the formula: my lip wedge.

Just when you think you've seen everything possible on a golf course, someone aces a short par three with a driver or somehow swings violently forward but hits the ball backward. At the golf course, the best equipment and name-brand attire can be distractions momentarily, until their owner unveils a bizarre swing. It's also where disheveled-looking folk with camouflage pants and self-tattoos can roll out of rusted Baja trucks and transform into Bobby Joneses as they strike their garage-sale persimmon woods on the first tee.

Most of us have no hope of gaining anything but enjoyment from playing this Renaissance game. The best four rounds of our lives, usually scored from closer tees than on TV and on lesser courses, wouldn't qualify us for any PGA tournament. Most of us, even those few scratch golfers among us, resonate more with hackers than hall-of-famers.

As Bagger Vance says, "Golf is not a game to be won, but only played. So I play on." And so do I—with a smile. And I'm sure I give my playing partners plenty to smile about as well.

Jerry Pattengale
Marion, Indiana, May 3, 2016

CHAPTER ONE

The FedEx Cup and Political Swings

First Place Award, Sports Writing—*Hoosier State Press Association, April 15, 2016 (for 2015)*

I have a Pelosi golf swing—always hitting the bushes. My Limbaugh follow-through isn't much better—a confident stance with unknown consequences. Of course, my Chomsky-Obama bunker play invites everyone into the same sand, and my Gore steel shafts have zero flex. My Dick Cheney driver may find the wrong target. And at our Donald Trump driving range, you can hit eleven million balls over the fence, and someone sends them all back.

American life is indeed linked to the links.

Golf affords us shared images and metaphors as pronounced as politicians' strengths and weaknesses. Major tournaments highlight unique personalities and players, from Furyk's knee-knocking swing and Jason Day's dreamy, preshot eyes to Villegas's spider position. Weekend golfers can nickname our shots after stars in the PGA or players in today's political forays. Or a bit of both.

For example, my Barbara Boxer fairway shots make friends smile—always radically left even on dogleg rights. My Greenspan putts are usually misread. And for some reason, my Robert Gibbs phone disappears when not silenced.

Golf is unpredictable. Like *Tin Cup*'s Roy McAvoy or Crooked Stick's John Daly, anyone can win. Our plebeian public courses have their own surprises, from the 30-handicapper getting an ace to the scratch golfer scoring a quadruple bogey.

Frontrunners can indeed surprise us, along with the weather. And if rain comes unexpectedly on our parades, there's the Hart *Monkey Business* slicker. If it's unusually arid at launch sites, we can use our Palin tees and drill those puppies in. The new Lindsey Graham Fitbit tracks steps between watering holes.

Golf is humbling. It's a leveling experience regardless of pedigree, from Henrik Stenson's Deutsche Bank collapse on the sixteenth, to the world's number-1 Jordan Spieth missing cuts in two FedEx playoff tourneys, and yet with a stellar sixteenth recovery in the Coca-Cola's third round from a Georgian woods.

My Clinton scorecard (non-clubhouse-issue) seems to minimize these situations by deleting strokes.

Yep, golf measures us. Integrity and patience are always on trial, especially off the beaten path in Bethpage Black's fescue.

My Arlen Specter caddy makes some drastic turns, and my George Will–Penick version of the *Little Red Book* turns heads with multisyllabic adjectives. And yes, I have Rick Perry–Buddy Holly glasses to spot good places to exit and extra pairs, called Boehners, for transitional golfers.

Golf is rewarding. It offers glimpses of momentary greatness regardless of the final score, such as Bill Haas's brilliant water shot in 2011 or Bubba's Masters' bender in 2012.

During scrambles we get to rest on others' laurels and use our Biden bags—carried by others. Of course my Huckabee mulligans keep me contributing to the game even after losing.

Golf is sometimes loud. The applause for Fowler's final round 38-foot putt at the Deutsche Bank was deafening, along with every romp down the sixteenth at TPC Scottsdale—ensconced by twenty thousand fans.

My thunderous Howard Dean golf cart squeals its tires. My partners' Bill Maher's lip wedges keep matters lively—ignoring all good shots while magnifying the bad.

My Gingrich SkyCaddie measures only the green's extremes, in detail. And there are usually memorable Ross Perot water shots and giant sucking sounds. My partner's Karl Rove cell phone constantly interrupts my swings with Wilson and Plame tweets.

Golf can be unforgiving. One lip out on the penultimate green can halt David Duval's noble 2008 U.S. Open run or Tom Watson's final hole in Scotland in 2009.

I have a Letterman golf towel—a freebee from an Alaskan law firm. My Blagojevich skins game has guaranteed foursomes. No worry, my Mitch Daniels golf budget has a $5 limit.

Yep, golf is revealing. Your equipment, like Scott's ephemeral belly putter, reflects your commitments.

My Larry King clubs emphasize diversity—some senior, oversized heads amid several young beauties. And my Ahmadinejad divots are huge and badly need replacement. However, my John Kerry backswing has me yelling "fore!" in advance, in several Arabic dialects.

The new Ben Carson Siamese-twin sand wedge is suddenly touted as able to dislodge a Republican ball from a Democratic trap. And with my Fiorina–Haney Blueprint, I "gain the advantage" by hearing women's input loud and clear.

Golf is public. The few minutes after Payne Stewart's 1999 U.S. Open victory are some of the most precious minutes ever filmed. His wardrobe also remains iconic.

There's also the Al Sharpton golf shirt, though the pocket hanky is tough to keep folded. If you stare long enough at my John Daly pants, I think you can see either Jesus, Bob Marley, or Miguel Jiménez. And my Rand Paul golf manual speeds the game by limiting the rules.

Yep, golf can and should be fun. We are reminded often that it's just a game. We've fallen in love with Fred Funk and Jerry Kelly for their playfulness, along with David Feherty's hair and Gary McCord's handlebars. Their self-effacement helps us to see our own faces more clearly.

My Jacobsen eraser is refreshing, especially when my CNN pencil keeps slanting. The groundkeepers' O'Reilly Round Up comes with a label on how things were actually killed. My 1-percent Rand Paul ball marker is replacing my bulkier Euro. And our Michael Breed–Jeb Bush briefcase is filled with hanging chads, coconuts, and other Florida novelties to ensure a *Golf Fix*. It also comes in Spanish and apologizes if it misspeaks to players' spouses.

Golf creates reference points. When the day is over, it's just a game. Phil Mickelson reminds us of this with his family-first choices. Any glimpse of Erik Compton on the course speaks to fortitude. It's a beautiful stage where public performance can accent private values in ways that touch a nation. Politics still has that possibility.

We have reference points like Quail Hollow's Green Mile, Riveria's Hogan's Alley, and St. Andrews's Swilcan Bridge. And we have the Lincoln Memorial, Arlington National Cemetery, the Old North Church, the Liberty Bell, and a host of common reminders of our great nation—from repurposed one-room schoolhouses that dot our countryside to church steeples and worn copies of King James Bibles and *Common Sense*. Similar to the way we watch golf, our lives can intersect from the fairway or the stands, through education, observation, or participation.

Perhaps politicians could learn from this irenic golf culture, where true character stands the test of time, where the measure of a participant is as much about what is done in private as what is displayed in public. We could use our modified John Oliver bullhorn—replaying the past week every Sunday afternoon. The modification? It bleeps the crass F-bomb, bizarrely applauded on HBO but considered appalling on the *Morning Drive.*

And golf is hopeful. I keep my Tiger Woods three-wood ready. Just when you think you've lost your game, there's his brilliant stinger that stuns the world. That singular club reminds me that barriers can be broken and that when rules and relationships are . . . in time broken hearts and reputations can be mended. I think I'll hand that club to a few feisty folk in the Capitol and on the campaign trail, even if it likely won't be used until after the FedEx Cup—and the primaries.

CHAPTER TWO

Teeing Off a Skunk on a Buck Creek Golf Course

He asked for advice on his club selection.

I replied, "The one you feel most comfortable with." It was my first time caddying. I had never golfed.

The pot-bellied businessman pulled out a two-iron, threw down his thin cigar, adjusted his polyester button-down, and swung away.

It was the shot of his life—powerfully sailing with a slight draw. It one-hopped to the front of the green, rolled slightly left, and nestled near the pin.

"Kid, you're a genius!"

My advice worked only once. For sixteen more holes, I lugged his overstuffed ostrich-skin bag and kept quiet. I spent a year on the course that day—for $4 and a used golf ball.

Until then, I had never entered the course gate—a stone boundary to nonmembers. It represented access to a country club, and we were country boys without clubs. Members drank fine wine. Our parents drank Falls City beer. Members drove shiny sedans and some smoked Tiparillos. We passed by in jerry-rigged trucks with gun racks and toolboxes while our dads smoked filterless Camels. Members worked wonders with Ping and Titleist, we worked with Craftsman and salvaged titles.

Financially and culturally, access to golf was unthinkable and undesirable.

I had been on that course one other time—long after sunset and over a side fence. The high school seniors took us "rookies" snipe hunting. The initiation passed quietly, except for one overzealous Buck Creek boy.

He yelled, "Snipe! Snipe!" and took off with his gunnysack. Hoopin' and hollerin,' he jumped toward it—only to become stunned by a foul spray. Whatever a snipe is, it is not white striped with a black tail. The upperclassmen abandoned the sorry-smellin' misguided-sniper. He had no luck hitchhiking either. After a few days of tomato-juice baths, he finally returned to the jeers of the school hallway.

While caddying, I was more interested in seeing the skunk-episode site in the daylight than replacing chunks of grass from my golfer's low swings. Every time, the guy tore up the expensive grass.

Golf courses were funny foreign places to my dad and uncles. Other than Cubs and Purdue games on garage radios, sports were not part of their tough lives and time-clocked weeks.

Access to college also seemed inaccessible and foreign.

Although Purdue was nearby, passing through campus could have been like traversing Oz—such a strange land. Except for a field trip to watch Bob Ford and Rick Mount practice, and a Christmas banquet, the college campus was someone else's world. I remember sitting in the front row in Mackey Arena in awe of a building that could house our town. The floor was eye level, and the players were giants. They were TV people. Little did I know that teachers were trying to show me the yellow brick road. Like organizers of Upward Bound, they understood the importance of breaking down a barrier—unfamiliarity—to the college experience.

A concerned school counselor, scholarships, and Pell-grant aid helped open the door. Through Mr. Brewer's history lectures at Harrison High School and a relentless recruiter—a self-imposed guardian of my college future—at sixteen I was on my way to Indiana Wesleyan University—then Marion College—with all bills paid.

Access is more than money; it's also a mindset. The applicant needs a desire and a plan, and an institution needs to plan for such desires.

New knowledge begged new answers. Mr. Brewer had an uncanny way of taking a simple unsparked mind and making it blaze. Suddenly my world opened to larger realities than grease guns and hunting seasons. For the first time, I wanted to learn beyond my situation. The lights went on, and I began to dream. I wanted to listen to this one-time college gibberish. Access started to mean opportunity. The opaque admission door turned transparent.

Like admission to the golf club, access included a mind-set—both for the potential member and the institution. College personnel pulled while those at the high school pushed. And somewhere in the process, I could grab hold.

Thirty years later, access has a new challenge—the financial aid door remains opaque. Students with a dream find it increasingly difficult to go through the door—no matter who is pushing and pulling.

For many communities, financial assistance isn't keeping pace with the tuition costs; students can't afford the membership fees. Compared to 1975, the Pell grant has about one-fourth the buying power for today's Buck Creek kids. Likewise, their parents cannot afford special SAT study courses or academic prep camps. In turn, their children will likely miss the best scholarships. Many of these kids are gifted students; they may gain access later in life—but after missing a decade of opportunities.

Access to college has led to fulfillment and fun in a rather complex and chaotic time. Most important, it's allowed me to understand my life calling, yes, a purpose-guided life.

There will always be exclusive clubs and colleges, but the mind-set I promote sees concerned golfers and academics striving to ensure access to the playing field at some level. My home course is not Pebble Beach, but it's my connection to such an experience, and for some gifted members to believe that Tiger's and Phil's world is within reach. Our college is not Harvard, but our students engage in the same life-changing dialogue, in the same "great debate" and with a clear mission.

A few years ago, I took a nine-year-old to the golf course. For the first time, he stood at a tee and swung. He lost eight of my balls in the second-hole pond. But like that pot-bellied businessman thirty years ago, he'll long remember that shot that sailed to the green (even if it was his twenty-sixth stroke). It was his personal experience, his struggle and eventual joy, from inside the gate. (He, Michael Moffitt, went on to high jump more than 7 feet in college and became a national champion.)

The next week, I took my seventy-two-year-old friend, Johnny Taylor, for his first round. He noted that he hadn't ever been invited earlier in life, presumably because he was African American. And yes, we sure laughed loudly at the second-hole pond. By the end of our round, he was swinging like Bubba Watson and exuded pure joy and fascination. It's a prized memory, as it proved to be his only course outing before his death a few months later.

The PGA has successfully launched programs to open its gates to the Buck Creek types, and to the young Johnny Taylors. Many groups are trying to do the same at colleges.

The *Dr.* title before my name dangles as a membership card to the academy, and the Arbor Trace card on my bag identifies membership in a club. I'm not good enough to get mad at a bad shot. On the other hand, I'm always hopeful that people get at least one. Just don't hit a skunk with a stick, because the smell will follow you for life.

CHAPTER THREE

Taking Paul Stookey on Our Double-Decker Golf Bus

Our 1958 Cadillac was a sweet ride that sported leather pleated seats and cone-shaped lights on long tailfins. Well, that sweetness soured when Dad removed the trunk to insert a homemade camper. We, indeed, were from deep within the woods near Buck Creek, Indiana.

When you're inside such a jerry-rigged contraption, you can almost forget there's a square aluminum-sided house following you. When we approached stoplights, I'd pretend to be reading; I'd shield my face with my hand.

Our car was like the Oscar Mayer wiener car, only different. It was more like the Bat Mobile with a right-angled hemorrhoid.

The funny thing is, we never used it for camping. I think Dad lost it in a poker game.

He built another beautiful camper to attach to a truck, even though we didn't have one. Once again it disappeared before we could camp. The third time was a charm; his conversion of an old Bluebird school bus was a different story. With ten in our family, it made a lot more sense, and we used it a couple of times—to haul us to Michigan to pick strawberries. We weren't migrant workers, but our vacations sure had that feel. All the way back to Buck Creek, we had to shimmy past hundreds of quarts of strawberries. Ah, we were fruit rich and fund poor.

This week I rode in another sleeper bus, but this time in style. No strawberry fields ahead, but bent grass and gorgeous fairways in Myrtle Beach, South Carolina. The double-decker sweet ride is owned by Lightrider Ministries in Upland, Indiana. Imagine eighteen grown men committing to a thirteen-hour bus ride. The symphony of snores. The laughter over euchre. The long wide-ranging chats. The smack-talking from golf hacks like me. The stops at Bob Evans for chicken potpie. Yes, it was bliss—and landed us in Myrtle Beach for five rounds of golf on great courses.

On the surface, the ride made little sense for me after accruing around two hundred thousand airline points that month. My travel agent asked why I didn't end my final flight in Myrtle Beach, since it was the same price as touching down in Fort Wayne. After all, it was the last leg of a bizarrely busy week. Google the *Huffington Post* and "C.S. Lewis College Flops," and you'll find me, a few days earlier, in the middle of the discussion in Northfield, Massachusetts. Or the *Boston Globe* and *Christianity Today*. For days my cell phone remained hot from fielding calls from readers interested in the story. From there to Atlanta meetings, then . . . the trip I had circled on my calendar. The trip that made me smile amid long days.

Finally, as I entered the bus, there was silence. I switched off my overused iPhone.

The star-spangled bus, a rolling testimony to Old Glory, became a mobile sanctuary.

The golfing proved great, well, everything except my swing and scores. But who really cared? I lost a dozen reused ProV1s, likely to be found, repackaged, and sold once again. I realized that golf was an excuse for a retreat we all needed. Engineers, managers, hourly employees, a gifted radio DJ. What a mélange of men. An eighty-year-old brilliant businessman who'll never officially retire. An educator and retired Vietnam helicopter pilot. A water-department supervisor—much my golfing superior, a water-damage expert even better. A constable. And the Lightrider bus owners in their own class—the Manganello twins.

The trip includes a daily devotional from twin Steve, a self-effacing gentle giant with retread jokes. Humility covers many shortcomings, which itself is endearing.

The end of his last devotional proved memorable. When he announced that he was closing with a song from Paul Stookey (of Peter, Paul, and Mary), I smiled. The above-mentioned then-current *Huffington Post* story involved some of Paul's friends, in his old Northfield neighborhood. His concert there is even cited in one of several articles.

My recollection of Paul's music was his famous "Wedding Song" ("There Is Love," 1971) and the much-misunderstood "Puff, the Magic Dragon" (1963). Where exactly did Puff live by the sea and frolic in "the land called Honah Lee"? Was it really just a children's song?

But Steve played neither of these famous tunes. Rather, he put the microphone to his iPod and then played Paul's 1968 gem titled "Hymn." The bus grew silent, the song demanding attention and reflection.

When it ended. More silence. Then the veteran pilot, a veteran friend, asked to hear it repeated; the lyrics especially resonated with his journey. Once again the double-decker Lightrider bus became a sanctuary. Lean forward and listen in to the lyrics:

Sunday morning, very bright,
I read Your book by colored light
That came in through the pretty
window picture.

I visited some houses where they said
that You were living
And they talked a lot about You
And they spoke about Your giving.
They passed a basket with some
envelopes;
I just had time to write a note
And all it said was "I believe in You."

Passing conversations where they
mentioned Your existence
And the fact that You had been replaced
by Your assistants.
The discussion was theology,
And when they smiled and turned to me

All that I could say was "I believe
in You."

I visited Your house again on Christmas
or Thanksgiving
And a balded man said You were dead,
But the house would go on living.
He recited poetry and as he saw me
stand to leave
He shook his head and said I'd never
find You.

My mother used to dress me up,
And while my dad was sleeping
We would walk down to Your house
without speaking,

I hope to sit for coffee with Noel Paul Stookey during one of my upcoming trips to Northfield, the birthplace of the famous D. L. Moody. From those sacred hills redound from very different men a similar message with different lyrics. In a sense, I suppose I'll have coffee with Paul hundreds of times in years ahead as I recreate that scene on that star-spangled sleeper bus. And I'll try to pay more attention to passing conversations.

My son and I saw the Oscar Mayer wiener car today as we drove to the Atlanta airport. There was no bizarre camper in our trunk, only luggage and the memory of a coffee chat.

Thanks Paul and also to those unique twins radical enough to invest their lives in the value of community—and a rolling sanctuary I'll rename Honah Lee.

CHAPTER FOUR

Crooked Stick Helped Me to Think Straight

The Crooked Stick PGA Champions tournament helped me to think straight. God's creation can be manicured beyond common imagination, and his created *Homo sapiens* can do amazing things through discipline. On the dogleg left hole 14, time stopped as Greg Norman stood over his fairway shot. Thousands of fans held their collective breath as the man in black did something I had only heard about—struck a ball with such fluidity and ease that it appeared to be caressed and not struck. The ball got in the way of his swing. Hardly a sound as it traveled 200 yards to a pampered landing on a complicated green. With fairways that could double as greens, cashmere greens with Princess Di presence, and manicured surroundings and damask rough, the cast of golfing legends proved perfect accents.

I wanted my son to ignore the glitz of the Lexus tent, the Rolex clocks, and the LCD attractions in the inviting Pete Dye tent. I hoped he and I would take in a full-sensory experience of humankind's efforts to craft our surroundings as well as our abilities, to exercise what many Christians call the "dominion mandate"—treating our environment and skills with honor and creative leadership. There on that Crooked Stick tournament stage, some of the best of both were manifest in stately brilliance. The grounds crew had spent years preparing the backdrop, and Greg Norman, Jay Haas, and Bernhard Langer even longer, preparing themselves.

Nearly all shots reminded me that not all men and women are created athletically equal; not all of us are called to a professional sports vocation. Nearly every turn reminded me that not all men and women are created creatively equal; not all of us are called to be horticulturalists. Even the LCD screens showing coverage of the event transpiring a few yards from the tent's windows reminded me that not all of us are created with the same engineering acumen or requisite technological skills; we're not all called to such a career. I believe that we're all better human beings when we understand these dynamics—when we can stand at the fairway ropes and recognize what's playing out before us.

Educated citizens need to recognize higher standards of accomplishment and also identify what resources and skills are needed to reach them. We're not all wired to be public political leaders, but all nominally educated citizens are required to recognize and demand the best of leaders in public. We're not all destined for financial excess, but to the best of our ability we're capable of financial responsibility.

We're not all positioned to be inside the fairway ropes, but we can know the ropes' purpose and why we're on one side and the Normans, Funks, and Watsons on the other.

I grew up in Buck Creek, Indiana, which boasted no manicured yards. Instead of John Deere mowers, we saw real deer--and pigmy goats as lawn keepers. No one hung fancy golf clubs in garages but, rather, prized torque wrenches for camshaft work. No Nike shoes lined up alongside the automatic garage door but, rather, steel-toed work boots near bulky manual swing doors. No one owned Wii golfing machines but, rather, a grease-covered radio with aluminum foil to boost reception of Brickyard races. I saw no cute putting contraptions that kick back balls, but we did rally around an old target with cheap plastic darts sticking randomly in the tool peg board.

Decades later I'm still on the outside of the fairway ropes, and my heritage is still inside the Buck Creek fences. But things are much different. I'm able to look at a man in a black brimmed hat perform amazing feats with a four-iron and recognize the moment's brilliance. Education has helped me to articulate what I sense and see, experiences that during my youth were unknown, let alone unprocessed. Kids in Buck Creeks worldwide may live out their days without ever doing so, and their lives can still be successful. But my hope is that they can recognize deeper meaning, pursue those vantage points to appreciate greatness, and learn from it.

One can live a full life but miss its fullness. Yeah, I'm a mediocre golfer at best, and any good shot is an aberration. I'll always be on the outside of the fairway ropes, but not on the outside of understanding.

Moments before I left the Crooked Stick course in the Indy suburbs, I watched Tom Watson tee off before tens of thousands. He looked old, more weathered than I had anticipated, and he was already sweat drenched before his first shot. But that snapshot moment of his gentle steel smile also showed me a majestic man who epitomized success in many ways.

Not all crowds gather at the ropes for the right reasons, but some ropes frame a moment where the good in our race races to the front. Education should help us all to have that chance: not at success in all areas but to recognize and appreciate success in any arena.

CHAPTER FIVE

Practical Jokes Are Par for the Course

The archaeologist at our excavation site near Corinth, Greece, was ecstatic; he had discovered a coin that would date the earliest classical temple ever found. But why were his colleagues from the University of Chicago laughing a few minutes later?

Imagine his dismay when he dug just a bit deeper in his trench near the temple's foundation and found a twentieth-century plastic button! The team's snickers betrayed its scheme.

Though I, working just down the hill in Isthmia with the National Endowment of Humanities team, missed that joke, I've been on the receiving end of many.

During my last class lecture at Miami University in Ohio, the other teaching fellows strategically placed an embarrassing item in my notes; the item literally fell into the lap of the male student in the front row. (It was not for males.)

Earlier classes that day were also targeted. My colleagues had taped a self-effacing sign on the bottom of my briefcase, which I always placed on the old wooden table with its bottom facing the class. For another class, they glued my notes together, and they also moved my car to a remote lot.

And I've been able to give, as well, including during a parents' day when I was teaching in California. Before one of my large history classes, without the student's knowledge, I gave his visiting father the answer key to that day's quiz. The student couldn't believe his father asked to take the quiz and nearly fainted when his father aced it!

In another class, I gave a parent answers to questions I would ask aloud in class, such as, "What Indian chief did Alexander the Great chase and catch, and in what year and area of India?" I almost needed Depends as I waited for an answer. No students raised their hands, but eventually the parent raised his. His son was rather embarrassed, that is, until his otherwise shy father waxed eloquent about King Porus on his elephant in the Punjab—and cited the ancient source!

My first day of teaching in California was also priceless. Rather young, I arrived early and sat in the audience while the 150 students filed in. The freshman next to me turned to chitchat, wondering where the prof was. Then he proceeded to tell me that he hated history, that it was likely going to be a terrible semester because some new dude was teaching, someone listed as "staff." When I stood and walked to the podium, he couldn't contain his shock, other than slapping his forehead and saying, "Well, I'm finished . . . Just give me an F!"

As the guest speaker at a Youth for Christ camp, I was asked to participate in a Jeopardy-type game during afterglow (a late-night light-hearted time after the campfire). The host was a fun but rather overconfident fellow, so I rationalized a humility, or maybe humiliating, strategy (and, forgive me, I was in my midtwenties). I located the question cards and changed every fifth or sixth answer. I'm laughing as I type this; it's still funny. Imagine trying to defend the written answer that Buck Owens was the all-time best-selling rock-and-roll recording artist. Or that Willie Nelson wrote and sang "You Light up My Life."

On another occasion, I was keynoting for a Wesleyan church camp in Illinois. My friend was responsible for, and rather proud of, the daily newsletter. Another mutual friend worked nearby and had access to the mimeograph machine. (Yeah, this goes back thirty years.) Imagine when people at breakfast began reading articles in *The*

Daily Blast (instead of *The Daily Bugle*), about a Wesleyan pastor (the newsletter's editor) winning a local dance contest. Here it helps to know the old joke that Wesleyans didn't believe in premarital sex because it might lead to dancing! Until now, folk have never known who produced the issue.

Years later and locally I spearheaded a trick played on the golden-voiced Jim Brunner at our Wednesday night golf outing. Our weekly Wednesday night league couldn't have better scripted his "innocent" comment. While I was giving introductory remarks, near the Arbor Trace clubhouse Jim rummaged through a tub of hundreds of "experienced" golf balls found on the course—usually in the ponds or woods. We had scribbled his initials on about a third of them. Without thinking, he said in his megaphone whisper, "Man, this JB fellow must be a terrible golfer!" Then he saw one with "WBAT–JB," then "Jimmy B," and "1400–JB." If I'm smiling when you visit me in the nursing home someday, you'll know what I'm thinking about. Either that, or the time we planted a professional sign "Keith Newman Memorial Woods" where an otherwise decent golfer lost a few balls. He got calls for months from people making sure he saw it!

Maybe he was lucky, I could have placed a mounted scorecard in the clubhouse, as we did in California before an annual tournament. It had a fake "record score" for the highest strokes ever—with our friend's name on it; David Bicker seemed to deserve a little ribbing. He played with the intensity of *Bourne Identity*, but with a swing like Jim Furyk with duct-taped arms, or a cross between Abe Vigoda and Jack Nicklaus playing in a dress shirt.

I suppose we like to laugh because life brings us plenty of sorrow. This week I spent time with a loved one going through sustained pain due to life choices. I also visited a funeral home, consoling family of a beautiful man who died all too young. And I grieved with great friends suffering the toughest of losses—a child—just a week after another university family lost a college son. Sad times for sure. This stretch was capped by news images from ISIS of twenty-one Coptic Christians about to be decapitated, the Copts being a group I've worked among as an archaeologist. Evil should always sadden our soul and strengthen our bent toward goodness.

The title of Focus on the Family's CD from Tim Keller seems appropriate, "Discovering God in the Midst of Pain and Suffering." Also, the words of Ecclesiastes 3:4, that there is "a time to weep and a time to laugh, a time to mourn and a time to dance." And further down, the passage "I know that there is nothing better than for people to be happy and to do good while they live" (v. 12 NIV).

Silliness and sorrow are sometimes minutes apart, but both are seasons for all of us to weather. Laughter doesn't eradicate loss, but it may eclipse despair. And at times it may facilitate our heart's repair. During years of navigating our sons' chronic diseases, silliness and sadness often hit in the same day. We also tried throughout, though not always successfully, to be attached to good causes, a faith-based remedy for finding happiness amidst hollowness.

These are tough times for so many, I know. But as life has demonstrated, there can still be times ahead for laughter. And personally, with golf season around the corner and my network of hackers still swinging, it'll sure be hard not to smile. Or for golf purists, not to cry.

CHAPTER SIX

Happy Thoughts from Former Fairways

Each morning as I teed off at Walnut Creek near Marion, Indiana, I would pause and absorb what I saw, "Heaven is kissing earth. Heaven is kissing earth."

The sprinklers would fade and the fog would linger on the raised green 360 yards straight ahead, framed by moguls and an undulated rough on the left and an elevated pond on the right. I often felt the need to pinch myself to make sure I wasn't dreaming. The billboard ad for the course is fitting: "Great golf courses aren't made but discovered."

This poor boy from Buck Creek seemed out of place in such confines. Beauty for me had been relegated to Ginger on *Gilligan's Island*, but this was a much richer experience. For starters, it was real.

Thirty-five years later, I can still feel the moist air and wet grass. I can see the trail of my partner's footprints up the slight hill to dip his towel in the pond to clean his clubs. I recall just as vividly the former starkly furnished clubhouse, the gravel parking lot, and the cheap coffee. The occasional deer on hole 2. The invasion of golf carts by the turn at hole 9. The grand old oak that once stood at the tenth green. The horses that were in constant danger to the left of the memorable downhill eleventh fairway. A young owner's megaphone voice as he greeted us.

And when my game left me, which usually was on tee 1, searching for balls was as addictive as mushrooming. The woods and creek near the twelfth to fifteenth holes seemed to produce Titleist gems. Some mornings it was as if God had given me solid-core manna with dimples. They dotted the banks like eggs at a kindergarten Easter egg hunt.

The course didn't change in those days, but I did. I shot a 76 and 96 on consecutive days. I started golfing there with a set of rusty Northwesterns from a Gas City garage sale, and ended using PGA blades from a scratch golfer. My spindly legs were still fresh. I carried my clubs, and the driving woods were still woods or replicas called metal woods. Today they are Rhode-Island on a stick and referred to as drivers and hybrids.

Harvey Penick and Payne Stewart were still alive. Tiger wasn't yet born, and my friend Herb Mohler was shooting in the sixties at the Lakeview course around the corner. Herb, near ninety, still shoots low scores over at the Arbor Trace league, but the Lakeview course is now an overgrown meadow. I can still shoot consecutive rounds twenty strokes apart, and the gregarious laughter of friends still rolls across the fairways, while some of their actions get us rolling across the fairway. My friend Terry Munday has got to be simultaneously the most sensitive, intense, and hilarious person in the county. Those aren't necessarily qualities for a good golfer but a good time while golfing!

We all need those Walnut Creek memories, those Peter Pan "happy thoughts" of *Hook* lore. And we all need an appreciation for seasons of life. Not bucket lists but lists of buckets filled with meaningful moments on this side of the daisies.

I'm writing this somewhere between Rome

and Madrid, at the end of a long week, to say the least. But I'm only as far away from Walnut Creek as a reflection. We all need happy thoughts, and we need reference points. Yesterday during a barrage of unfortunate media about my role in a Bible project, a friend called and gave me one of those very reference points, from the Bible itself: "Surely the righteous will never be shaken; they will be remembered forever. They will have no fear of bad news; their hearts are steadfast, trusting in the LORD" (Psalm 112:6–7 NIV).

The second reference point was a quotation from John Wesley, fitting for someone still hours from boarding a plane en route back to the friendly confines of Indiana Wesleyan University. "Do all the good you can. By all the means you can. In all the ways you can. In all the places you can. At all the times you can. To all the people you can. As long as ever you can."

These days I've added the fifteenth to seventeenth holes at Arbor Trace Golf Course to that happy-thought list, but I think I'll make an overdue pilgrimage to Walnut Creek's first hole in the morning. I can already hear the owner's megaphone voice.

CHAPTER SEVEN

Jordan Spieth and I Shared a Quadruple

While Jordan Spieth was quadrupling hole 12 at the Masters, I was recovering from a quadruple bypass in Marion, Indiana, Jim Gallagher Jr.'s hometown. The doctors had just fixed my heart, but the Golden Bell had just broken Spieth's. The doctors saved my life. Hole 12 and Rae's Creek likely gave his life more meaning.

There's no consolation for Spieth in knowing that Tom Weiskopf shot a 13 on the same hole in the 1980 Masters or that Rae's Creek factored into the legendary Masters collapse by Greg Norman.

The amazing thing is that Spieth, at age twenty-two, shot a 7 on that hole and still finished second—and he showed resilience. Although his metal shafts let him down, his personal mettle was artfully on display. No clubs thrown in the water. No cursing a camera in the crowd. No blaming the caddy. And though he appeared numb during the green jacket ceremony, he saluted Danny Willett, the victor.

I became a Spieth fan because of the twelfth hole. While he lost a lot, his longtime gains will be greater. People admire talent but respect humility and grace. Speaking of losses, each water ball on hole 12 cost him $460,000—a total of $920,000 (a staggering amount in its own right, but also within $10,000 of half of Arnold Palmer's total career earnings over fifty-three years and 734 starts). But it wasn't about the money.

And Jordan, if you're reading, let me share that we have more in common than a quadruple. I also collapsed on the twelfth hole in the biggest tournament of my life—okay, the only actual tournament I've entered.

When I hit three balls into the same pond on hole 12, I realized my score in our club championship just went down the drink. When I hit four balls into it the next day during the tourney's second round, I started looking around for *Psycho*'s Norman Bates or *Harry Potter*'s Lord Voldemort—"I must be cursed."

I was having an out-of-body experience in front of club members. And it's not like you can hide your scores, which are immediately posted on Facebook. In about ten minutes across the two days I earned a scarlet letter—my clumsiness writ large a huge scarlet *7*.

To accent my misfortunate, they were ProV1s—that's $4 per ball times seven. In rapid succession both days, I was like a hay bailer feeding the retirement fund of ninety-year-old Jimmy Rice, who has dredged that pond for lost balls for decades.

And to make it worse, I had marked each ball with my initials! I wanted to sneak back and throw a couple of dozen balls into the pond with other members' initials—just to minimize my idiocy when Jimmy counted his booty.

Scoring an 11 on hole 12 the second day, I limped in with an 88. My colleagues invited me to play that same course later that day, which I did with my wife's blessing (sympathy). I birdied hole 12. And the next time I played it, I birdied it again and shot a 77. But not during that big tourney. No. No. There was more chance of one of the Kardashians appearing on *Focus on the Family* than of me avoiding the water.

While hitting those balls into the water, it was as if my arms were sides of frozen beef somehow affixed to me with bungee cords as I tried swinging them toward the green. I hit seven balls a total of 50 yards. The PGA pros can use the same type of pitching wedge to hit one ball 150 yards or more. I should have used rosary beads instead.

My mitigated disaster prompted "worst golf story" e-mails and chats. I think the winner (or loser) goes to my friend Bob. His friend got sick during an Arizona tourney—dehydration followed by diarrhea. During an emergency stop behind cacti along the fairway, he dropped his drawers but slipped, stumbled, and sat on a cactus. Suddenly my struggle at the pond didn't seem very painful.

After the 2016 Masters, millions of e-mails and posts surfaced about Augusta National's hole 12. Only four people saw my collapse. Hundreds of millions will see Jordan's—in high definition that will play long after his golf days are over. But these clips will also show that he birdied the next hole, and then 15 and almost 16. Long after I'm pushing up daisies, the Golf Channel will be running historic reflections, and, yes, Jordan's 2016 introduction to Rae's Creek will be included. But the clips will also show his lack of outbursts. His ability to navigate the ceremonies afterward. His ownership of the moment.

There's one more stinging aspect in the soggy saga of my golfing woes. I've had one hole in one, and it was just two months before my water episode. Guess where it was? Yep, hole 12 at Arbor Trace! The same infamous hole. Acing something in the past doesn't guarantee protection from a future gaff, and the success often accents mistakes all the more. Spieth's spectacular performances render his two errant shots sensational.

I'm fortunate to be alive. And if my hunch is right, I'll get to enjoy seeing a stoic twenty-two-year-old really begin to live.

BUCK CREEK series:
True Stories to Tickle Your Mind

The best from the funny newsprint series
by the Accidental Author!

215 Pages

Some books like *Buck Creek* have a buzz about their release. After all, it's not everyday someone rides a wild deer down the freeway against traffic. Some new books have fun news releases about them. In the case of *Buck Creek*, Why not? After all, it is a bit unusual for a scholar to publish books about school pranks and ancient manuscripts simultaneously, or to host a lecture series at the Vatican while people halfway across the world are reading his story about killing his uncle's giant hog. And some books take over a decade to write. *Buck Creek's* stories were released over twelve years through Jerry's newspaper column: articles about life in the sleepy town of Buck Creek, Indiana – true stories that tickled their minds. Actually, he likely had a sleepless childhood, raised deep in the adjacent woods in an energetic family of ten with little money. The seeds of that *Buck Creek* adventurousness sprouted into his full-bloomed creativity that assists his international career. A few of the stories have already appeared in major publishing venues, or have been read before large audiences. This is the first of the four *Buck Creek* books, and the newsprint series continues; you'll often find him laughing aloud in some plane as he recalls another story while writing his weekly column. *Buck Creek* also comes with a summary section after each story—whether for personal reflection or to discuss with others. Either way, if you're like his newspaper readers you'll probably find yourself retelling a few of these bizarre gems: all true, and with a reflective twist.

"Reading Jerry Pattengale is my favorite form of reality therapy. It's cheaper than psychoanalysis—and a lot more fun."

~ John Wilson
Editor, Books & Culture

BUCK CREEK:
True Stories to Tickle Your Mind

Available at:
www.DustJacket.com

Christmas Stories from the BUCK CREEK series...

48 Pages

This is another book from the Buck Creek newsprint series, focused entirely on the Christmas holiday. These were also published in a full-color, full-page series in newspapers on successive days. In other words, they are a big hit with the series readers. This book is one of more than twenty written by Jerry Pattengale (PhD, Miami, OH), who likes to golf, but isn't very good. He enjoys fishing, but no longer owns a pole. He loves music but is likely tone deaf. He enjoys sports but has asthma. And, he loves dogs but is allergic to them. Fortunately, he's not allergic to his keyboard and has tickled the ears of his readers for a couple decades, that is, when he's not engaged with more scholarly work. This year alone, six books are going to press, including one with Brill Publishing (Leiden) that includes original translations of fourteen Dead Sea Scrolls (co-edited with the eminent Emanuel Tov).

He also speaks internationally on educational and ancient research topics, and has appeared in various televised, radio and printed interviews. His mantra is the fulcrum of his work presented in his McGraw-Hill books, "The dream needs to be stronger than the struggle."

"To many Hoosiers, Jerry Pattengale has become the Garrison Keillor of their beloved state. Take, read, smile, laugh and, when done, leave Jerry's work on the doorstep of a hardened enemy (if needed, I fear I can loan you one or two). You'll soon make a friend and experience a good measure of the Christmas joy reflected in these pages."

-Todd Ream *teaches at Taylor University and has called the Hoosier State home for over a decade*

45075831R00038

Made in the USA
Middletown, DE
24 June 2017